VOLUME 103 OF THE YALE SERIES OF YOUNGER POETS

It Is Daylight

Arda Collins

Foreword by
LOUISE GLÜCK

YALE UNIVERSITY PRESS / NEW HAVEN & LONDON

Copyright © 2009 by Arda Collins.
Foreword copyright © by Louise Glück.
All rights reserved. This book may not be reproduced, in whole or in part, including illustrations, in any form (beyond that copying permitted by Sections 107 and 108 of the U.S. Copyright Law and except by reviewers for the public press), without written permission from the publishers.

Designed by Mary Valencia.
Set in Monotype Fournier type by Duke & Company, Devon, Pennsylvania.
Printed in the United States of America.

Library of Congress Cataloging-in-Publication Data
Collins, Arda, 1974–
It is daylight / Arda Collins ; foreword by Louise Glück.
p. cm. — (Yale series of younger poets ; v. 108)
ISBN 978-0-300-14887-9 (cloth : alk. paper) — ISBN 978-0-300-14888-6 (pbk. : alk. paper)
I. Title.
PS3603.O452618 2009
811'.6—dc22   2008040326

A catalogue record for this book is available from the British Library.

This paper meets the requirements of ANSI/NISO Z39.48-1992 (Permanence of Paper).
It contains 30 percent postconsumer waste (PCW) and is certified by the Forest Stewardship Council (FSC).

10   9   8   7   6   5   4   3   2   1

CONTENTS

Before Eddie Murphy became a movie star, he was a crucial part of one of the several golden ages of *Saturday Night Live;* I am thinking in particular of the beaming malice of Mr. Robinson (aka Mr. Rogers) of *Mr. Robinson's Neighborhood.* Here were all the accustomed props to which we parents were unavoidably exposed: the cardigan waiting in the closet (along with the comfy footwear constituting the at-home uniform that separated the outside from the inside); the new word chalked on the handy blackboard (a word that America's children were encouraged to both learn and visualize), the blackboard itself Mr. Rogers' solemn promise to parents that the children committed to his care were not transformed by the trance-inducing hypnotic screen into robots, but rather into readers. Unlike Mr. Rogers, Mr. Robinson was not at home; he was either staging a passive-aggressive refusal to vacate or he was practicing a vocation for hiding out; in either case, his visitors were enraged landlords. For a certain number of years, Fred Rogers' soothing chatter mutated on late-night TV into Mr. Robinson's solitary paranoid ramblings: Mr. Robinson was unwelcome, but Mr. Robinson, for the benefit of all of us former children too hooked or wired to go to sleep, Mr. Robinson was digging his heels in and, crouched under the window, ready to talk, even if talking meant talking to a void.

What these segments have in common with Arda Collins' savage, desolate, brutally ironic first book is the electric excitement of a master performance conducted in a deliberately isolated space, as though isolation were a form of control that promoted fluency. Like Eddie Murphy, Collins has invented a persona: *Welcome to my world,* the first poem seems to say, and for the next ninety-two pages, we are her mesmerized audience—nobody escapes:

> At last, terror has arrived.
> Next door, the house has gone up in flames.
> A woman runs from the burning wreck, her face smeared
> with blood and ashes. She screams that her children are kidnapped.
> It's truly exciting, and what more would anyone ask?
> For a rare and beautiful egg to present itself in the grass?
> For sex with the liquor store owner to progress into something meaningful?
> You don't know what I've done in front of the mirror.
> I've pulled my shorts up high like a thong. I've walked back and forth
> doing little kicks and making faces. I've stopped, I've stared.

I try to get my mind around the sight of myself. I make a face.
Of great seriousness. I imagine that I've just received
a large and upsetting piece of news. Then I look into my eyes.
Can I guess what I am thinking? Can I tell you what it is?
        —"The News"

It Is Daylight has, to some extent, roots in those long Victorian monologues in which character is developed through manipulation of tone, and a narrative emerges through that character's evasions and juxtapositions. A closer analogy might be the analytic monologue (though Collins' brilliant, sly free associations are far more original than the patient is ever likely to be). Structurally, the poems resemble not adult analysis as much as the work done with children, in which dramatic play augments or provides occasions for speech. The analytic perspective contributes detachment, distance; the self that acts is, here, always at a certain remove, its actions observed with a committed neutrality. Collins talks without interruption (no one is ever present to interrupt); she also performs, exhibits herself. But make no mistake: this is not a book of individual travail and self-exposure. Like the analyst, these poems never stop thinking. Collins' mugging and kicking are the opposite of narcissistic preening; they arise, I think, out of deep confusion. The parading in front of mirrors, like the invisible quotes around "meaningful," like the elliptical memories and tableaux, the fantasies—all dramatize a fundamental vacancy: the hope is that one of these gestures, one of these stories, will seem authentic, representative.

At the heart of the poems' struggles is shame, which results not from something the speaker has done, from action, but rather from *being*, from what she is or what she lacks. Collins' speaker cannot bear to be seen; hence her furtiveness, her preference for enclosed environments (sometimes her fear of light). The private closed spaces that protect this speaker from being seen (while paradoxically freeing her to speak) function in other ways, both contextualizing and mirroring a metaphysical claustrophobia: the bleak fate of being always one person. Sometimes Collins' closed space is not merely contained but barely plausible, the space of a human foot on top of a slice of onion:

As you're standing with the heel of your shoe
on top of some neatly sliced red onion
you might think to yourself, "I'm at onion,"
or, "I'm in onion today." Coming home
in the evening you might see a letter

waiting there, tucked just underneath
the sliced onion. . . .

and later:

. . . That evening, beside the onion,
you write in your journal . . .

As the poem goes on, as less of the world comes in, disorientation intensifies:

. . . You sleep
on the floor and wake
disoriented and frightened, uncertain if
the heaviness surrounding your sleep is onion
that still permeates your fingers. Day comes
to your estranged bed,
the mood of the bathtub inexplicably
altered . . .
　　　—"With A Voice In Front Of You"

Many poems follow the same arc: what begins as reprieve ends as indictment. The poems are ruled by habit, by ritual, their speaker less hostage to a specific secret than constrained by the habit of secrecy, the need to be protected from the unknown. She understands from the inside the prison of magical thinking; in one poem, she cannot decide "which way to walk around / and approach the table / for the best outcome."

Ritual and hiding promise safety; so too does art, which excludes the world, constructing a parallel and at least partially sustaining universe. But art is dangerous, taunting; it exposes insufficiencies; it takes one to the terrible depths one fears:

Don't put off your shower any more
listening to Chopin.
Take the Preludes personally;
he's telling you that he can describe a progression
that you yourself have been unable to see,
shapely, broad light at one-thirty,

evening traveling up a road,
an overcast day as gentle bones.
Don't remember the music;
remember it as something obvious
that you are compelled, doomed, to obscure
and complicate. You erase it twice.
The first time
as you listened, unable
to have it,
the second time
as you were unable
to remember it.
Angry with Chopin,
what does he know? . . .

and finally:

Listen to him describe what you would be like
if you were blind, sitting in a chair, at a wake, the days short, that there might
    be nothing
else, night,
content, unable, unwishing, to recall desire, or sight.
    —"Not For Chopin"

This locked-in quality, the inescapability of self, manifests temporally as well as spatially.
"It Is Daylight" constructs a universe in which time doesn't pass; in one poem, the accident
of stepping on an onion elaborates itself into a version of Dickinson's letter to the world.
And in the book as a whole, time has ceased, though day flips into night and back again, like
two aspects of paralysis. Because the self doesn't change, because it is exposed to nothing
that would change it, time seems not to pass. The last poem recapitulates the first, with its
burning house and kidnapped or murdered child—all these poems later, we're still frozen
in front of the television, watching these same images. Or this is a version of the onion-
world: a book-length account of a moment. The passion not to be seen is played back in
the poems as intense seeing, voyeurism; the "estranged bed," i.e., the world, intrudes, via
television, into Collins' Skinner boxes.

But no description of prevailing atmosphere does justice to Collins' achievement. How has she managed to make, out of stasis, a book so intensely dramatic? The obstacles are obvious: if the voice deviates too much from narrowness, then narrowness seems willed, artificial; the reader's belief falters. But the obsessive precisions that immobility is likely to produce seem, by definition, repetitive, boring. Collins' solutions are subtle: like a great actor, she stays in character; what moves is the camera:

It's not happiness, but something else; waiting
for the light to change; a bakery.

It's a lake. It emerges from darkness into the next day surrounded by pines.
There's a couple.

It's a living room. The upholstery is yellow and the furniture is walnut.
They used to lie down on the carpet

between the sofa and the coffee table, after the guests had left.

The cups and saucers were still.

Their memories of everything that occurred took place
with the other's face as a backdrop and sometimes

the air was grainy like a movie about evening, and sometimes there was an ending
in the air that looked like a scene from a different beginning,

in which they are walking.

It took place alongside a scene in which one of them looks up at a brown rooftop
early in March. The ground hadn't softened.

One walked in front of the other breathing.
The other saw a small house as they passed and breathed. The
    reflections in the windows

made them hear the sounds on the hill: a crow, a dog, and branches—
and they bent into the hour that started just then, like bending to walk under branches.
    —"Low"

As single moments expand to fill a page, memories (the *before* and *after* absolute but the transition nearly invisible) turn dreamy, partial. They seem less comprehensive anatomies than gestures or sketches, searches for analogues and tonal equivalents. By virtue of being past change, the world of memory, like the four walls to which Collins clings, makes an alternative to the outside world—here also time is banished, its repeated passage, phrase by phrase, controlled by the mind. But the world of memory remains strangely incomplete, elusive, mysterious, as though the poet cannot quite say what occurred, only what feelings were generated. The search is for exact emotion, not narrative fact—fact, to Collins, is suspect, a disguise; only nuance, the suggestiveness of a phrase, seems to her reliable, trustworthy. In a lesser poet this privileging of the evanescent over the concrete might be a dangerous predilection, but Collins' animal accuracies, her instinct and intelligence, never fail her. The respite of memory rewrites the schism in the self. The self in the present, always both performing and taking notes, becomes the self that acted and the self that remembers, the shift in tense making each self potentially whole. This, together with the atmosphere of searching or incompleteness, makes, despite the poem's sadness, a model for hope. If something can end (the *before* of *before* and *after*), something can begin; time can begin, feeling can begin.

Readers of these poems may think of Berryman's *Dream Songs,* though Berryman is more haunted by guilt than by shame. It is interesting to remember that those Dream Songs were followed by prayer: *Love and Fame* ends with a series of addresses to the Lord, which continue to seem to me among that poet's most moving work. Collins has woven theological argument (if not prayer) into her book; its thematic prominence intensifies as the book evolves. God is, in many instances, the only other presence, too mysterious and pervasive for any pronoun, divine authority confirmed by silence:

> I put my hands on the table
> and spread them, like
> "here's all ten." There's nothing on it,
> on the table,
> so I found that out.
> What did you do today?
> I ask god.
> God doesn't say anything.
> I don't say anything else. . . .

and later:

We stay like that
for a long time,
and I mean a really long time.
That's one thing,
god is the only one
who would do that.
　　　—"Heaven"

This conversation continues elsewhere with fervor: "The universe is on earth," Collins
writes, "unexpurgated / soil and frost." And the lament that has been fended off finally
surfaces, the persona splintering into the third person. "Dawn" is longer than many of these
poems, but its individual sections suggest, in their terse completeness, utter despair:

He slit a zoo
full of animals.
It was only one calf.
It turned out to be a person,
not a calf. The calf
made sounds.
Blood filled the grass,
the end of winter. . . .
　　　—"Dawn"/1

And then, from this persona-once-removed, an intelligence two voices away from the poet,
comes authentic grief, what is left when rage is played out:

Gentle, painful sound,
it's coming from his face.
He doesn't want to talk,
hates the air; it moves towards the same things,
beautiful night,
beautiful night again, best missed
from afar. . . .
　　　—"Dawn"/11

Collins is hopeless on principle: fear of disappointment combined with a vivid sense of helplessness have produced terror of action. For action, she substitutes memory and fantasy. Scrupulous inertia cannot, however, suppress an imagination so violently alive. The self that hides out is in fact a guerilla fighter; the atmosphere of the book is fierce engagement and despair, not placid resignation. The long, sometimes fragmentary poems of the book's second half do not represent disintegration. As paralysis and stasis substitute for wholeness or coherence, fragmentation manifests mobility. "Dawn"'s separation of rage from grief, as well as its somnambulistic quality, prepare for "Neptune." Here every line is succinct, but sequence, which earlier seemed fated, decided a priori, seems suddenly in flux. The beautiful phrases have a kind of stunned quality, a sense of being led forward, which oddly seems, in this context, freedom, since its alternative is adamant will wholly bent on repudiation:

> We pass the day in March of being in the cemetery and
> eating a burger.
>
> The air is made out of statues and dead people.
>
> This is why we have sex together.
>
> Did I show you this?
>
> It passed through the particles.
>
> The shadows of a continent passed over
> us like the shadow of a cloud over a body of water.

And later:

> The upstairs room in the summer is soft and quiet.
>
> Rain dims coming in the night outside.
>
> It is real that it is quiet, and the noise
> is away from here, inside the train.
>
> When I lie next to you I miss the world.

This is a book of dazzling modernity as, say, Jim Jarmusch seems modern: caustic, pithy, ruthlessly sharp witted and keen eyed, restless, devoid of that taste for rhetorical splendor that turns so easily stodgy. If the persona here is well defended, the larger point is that these defenses are among Collins' subjects. I know no poet whose sense of fraud, the inflated emptiness that substitutes for feeling, is more acute. Collins sounds always like a particular person, but she is, here, tracking a culture.

Within its devised constrictions, this voice has the freedom to say anything. The result is a book of astonishing originality and intensity, unprecedented, unrepeatable:

> There was snow on the apples
> somewhere.
> You're at home.
> It's getting dark out, rain
> makes the cars louder. Nobody
> seems to be driving
> the cars. Someone has arranged
> for them to be there going by,
> six o'clock. Someone has made
> the sound of air in the room louder.
> God? you say, but not aloud. Since
> there is no god, you have to be
> both you and god. . . .

The TV's on, "something about a fire / and a kidnapped boy." The hypnotic story unfolds again, the mother's anguish this time more detailed, more relentless. And then:

> . . . Her voice makes you hungry.
> You ask god if god
> is hungry, and god is. You ask god
> what you should do
> for dinner, and god reminds you
> that you have turkey burgers
> in the freezer, and some broccoli.
> You'll get up
> with creases on your face.
> The windows will be dark. You'll
> go take the burgers out

and separate them with a knife.
They'll be slippery and frozen, and
you'll think of driving on an
icy road; and then
you'll put them in foil under
the broiler and start the water
for the broccoli, and take out
a plate for yourself, and get
the salt and pepper, and by
that time god will have left.
God's going to a dinner
where they're having lamb chops
and veal stuffing with
roasted almonds and fig sauce and
Brussels sprouts buttered with pistachios.
And after, they're going to have
pear clafoutis behind a velvet curtain
and drive their skulls into the center of a diamond.
    —"Snow On The Apples"

Louise Glück

ACKNOWLEDGMENTS

Grateful acknowledgment is made to the editors of the publications in which these poems have appeared:

The American Poetry Review: "January"
"Snow On The Apples"
"Spring"
Canarium: "Central Park South"
"Pennsylvania"
The Canary: "Over No Hills"
"Poem"
GutCult: "A History Of Something"
"Pool #3"
"Pool #10"
jubilat: "The News"
"Heaven"
Make: "Arctic Poem"
"Elegy"
Moonlit: "With A Voice In Front Of You"
"Pool #13"
"Letter Poem #5"
The New Yorker: "Low"
"Not For Chopin"
A Public Space: "It Is Daylight"

Thank you to Louise Glück, the Iowa Writers' Workshop, Glenn Schaeffer, the International Institute of Modern Letters, and my teachers for their support and advice, and thank you to my family and my friends.

The News

At last, terror has arrived.

Next door, the house has gone up in flames.

A woman runs from the burning wreck, her face smeared

with blood and ashes. She screams that her children are kidnapped.

It's truly exciting, and what more would anyone ask?

For a rare and beautiful egg to present itself in the grass?

For sex with the liquor store owner to progress into something meaningful?

You don't know what I've done in front of the mirror.

I've pulled my shorts up high like a thong. I've walked back and forth

doing little kicks and making faces. I've stopped, I've stared.

I try to get my mind around the sight of myself. I make a face.

Of great seriousness. I imagine that I've just received

a large and upsetting piece of news. Then I look into my eyes.

Can I guess what I am thinking? Can I tell you what it is?

Spring

I was making a roast.
The smell wafted from the kitchen into the living room,
through the yellow curtains and into the sunlight.
Bread warmed in the oven,
and in my oven mitt, I managed to forget
that I'd ever punched someone in the face.
It seemed so long ago, I might not even have done it.
I went out into the yard before dark
and saw last year's rake on the lawn.
It was a cheap metal one
that tore up the old grass.
I did that for a while.
When I went back in the house,
the roast was burned black
and the bread was hard.
I sat on the couch and watched it get dark.
I was getting hungry, but I felt afraid
of seeing the refrigerator light go on.
Then I would have to turn on other lights,
and then what would I do?
I heard a car pass once in a while.
I thought about a time on vacation
when I bought a newspaper and tomatoes
from a supermarket I'd never heard of.

I remembered an old bathing suit I had,

but I couldn't think of what happened to it.

I could move away.

I could get in the car right now

and drive all night,

as soon as I had a sandwich.

Turkey, tomato, mayo,

Swiss, lettuce. It was exciting.

I still had my shoes on. I drove to a truck stop.

It was bright inside and I loved the world.

I bought a sandwich and ate it from my lap while I drove.

When I pulled up to my house it was quiet.

Pool #3

When I hear the ice cream man coming
Turkey in the Straw playing coming around
the corner, I duck
under the window curtains.
I peek at a bit of grass and the street
under the small apples on the hems.
I don't come out until he's gone;
I'm amazed at how still
I always am, but all the time I'm thinking
about the dollar bills in my wallet;
picturing myself out there next to his white truck;
buying a King Cone;
looking at the pictures of the ice creams
on a deep blue background;
reading the names and descriptions
of all of them, each one
shown with a bite out of it
so you can see what the inside looks like.
I would like to do this with people
so that I can see all the swimming pools inside them.
I'm hiding because *I don't want*
the ice cream man *to see my swimming pools.*

With A Voice In Front Of You

As you're standing with the heel of your shoe
on top of some neatly sliced red onion
you might think to yourself, "I'm at onion,"
or, "I'm in onion today." Coming home
in the evening you might see a letter
waiting there, tucked just underneath
the sliced onion. You would stand
with the heel of your shoe just beside
the slices while opening it. The letter
might be from a friend, filled with
some news, and asking how are you?
at your new place. A fly might come
in the window and land nearby
as you read. That evening, beside the onion,
you write in your journal, "Cloudy again.
A fly came to onion earlier; no other
visitors. Received letter from R. Stood
for several hours. Heard something fall
over and scatter outside at lunch time. Plan
to stay at onion
until the end of the month." You sleep
on the floor and wake
disoriented and frightened, uncertain if
the heaviness surrounding your sleep is onion

that still permeates your fingers. Day comes

to your estranged bed,

the mood of the bathtub inexplicably

altered; the smell of the darkened kitchen, the morning

hallway, the evening chairs. Alone

on the couch in the daytime you say something

aloud, and it's not your own voice that carries

through the living room, but a voice

that comes from in front of you and everything moves towards it.

The Sound Of Peeling A Potato

Polished shoes, and the world shines in them like a heaven.

Green grass on a sunny November afternoon

and the Leaning Tower of Pisa just in sight.

A low thump close to the ground

just before dark over some hills,

talking to someone in your head

who bears witness to your thoughts.

Lovers at a wintry lake

covered at night with snow.

The car pulled up so close to the edge.

Cold in black relief. Small cabins in a circle.

What will happen?

They'll wait five hundred years

while they sit and listen to a potato being peeled.

Not for all the blue sky will they know,

not for all the summer grasses, not for the creamiest cheek

that turns its lips the same forever for a lover on train over a hillside.

Low

It's not happiness, but something else; waiting
for the light to change; a bakery.

It's a lake. It emerges from darkness into the next day surrounded by pines.
There's a couple.

It's a living room. The upholstery is yellow and the furniture is walnut.
They used to lie down on the carpet

between the sofa and the coffee table, after the guests had left.

The cups and saucers were still.

Their memories of everything that occurred took place
with the other's face as a backdrop and sometimes

the air was grainy like a movie about evening, and sometimes there was an ending
in the air that looked like a scene from a different beginning,

in which they are walking.

It took place alongside a scene in which one of them looks up at a brown rooftop
early in March. The ground hadn't softened.

One walked in front of the other breathing.
The other saw a small house as they passed and breathed. The
        reflections in the windows

made them hear the sounds on the hill: a crow, a dog, and branches—
and they bent into the hour that started just then, like bending to
        walk under branches.

Department Store

You're a realist. It's a department store.
God is never there,

even when everyone goes home at night.

A saleswoman left her dark gray wool skirt
laid out on a chair when she went to bed.

The room was quiet while the woman slept.
The skirt didn't pray.

The skirt was lined with shadows from the blinds.
The lines moved around the room through the night.
The saleswoman breathed into the shadows.
Her breath, the heat, the faint smell of supper
she had made earlier passed through the skirt.

It was a long time since any speaking
but it was as though there had been speaking.

Night was long and day began forever.
The skirt was different than the night before.

A History Of Something

For the pilgrims, turkey was what was in style.
They dressed up like guns.

Tonight, it's macaroni with oregano,
tomato, and ham, and the kitchen light
comes from the butter and cheese. You're
sitting where you always sit. Every night
at dinner you're sitting with
the phrase "down the hall," because
you look down at the dark hall
from your chair at the kitchen table
and wonder if it's snowing.

Your toes turn a certain way
and you say, "ears."
You sit on the floor
and try to play cards, but
before you know it,
you're smushing the Jack
of Diamonds and the Queen
of Hearts together and
making them have sex and also
making the Queen of Clubs
watch, thinking, Jack's got that

weird little beard I always knew
he was up to no good—
the Jack of Hearts
would never do it with the Queen of Spades she's
in a totally different plotline wait
till the king finds out.

You go to your piano lesson. You
stink. You try to play,
"Surrey With The Fringe
On Top," for the entire
no one that will ever listen.
Walking home
at twilight, the city
buses you have no reason to ride,
you feel immoral,
just from walking
in the cold, smelling something
like smoke, and maybe if you
had a bus routine,
where you waited, and used quarters
to buy just rice to eat for dinner,
you'd be closer to god?

Letter Poem #5

Dear Turning Black,

I went to see the hypnotist
the other night
and all the next day
into the night that followed.
I've just come from there,
I think. The sun is coming up.
I'm watching a movie about winter.
Two people are walking across a snowy field at twilight.
In my room, too,
it's winter, can see my breath in bed, cold on the windows.
In the night I saw myself in the mirror
as though I had Down's syndrome, or a stroke,
wondered how I could still think,
where myself had gone to
to leave behind this slack-faced person,
incogent with a heavy lip,
thinking with a limp.
I must be inhabiting you
someplace close to here—
out in the part of this cold morning
that's visible
and the rest of this cold morning

that isn't, for miles;

how am I supposed to see for miles?

from in here?

how am I supposed to see with you in the middle of me?

25A

A little, wood statue
of Buddha, that you can't help
but see as a drunk, old
grandpa, with corn in his teeth.
So you go to the hospital, just
to visit his son. But then
you have to go every day
for weeks, and things keep
changing. Christmas comes
before you know it, and it's
backyard footprints in the snow
from the window, and grandpa's
yelling at you, as though
he's channeling
some asshole from another
century, who still wants
to get his licks in somehow.
The icy harbor, plaid.
And then it's not Christmas anymore
but it still gets dark early, headlights
on at four; they come toward you going
"Hurry home!" You
just want to kill yourself, but
no, you don't want to

kill yourself? You pass

a nursery on your way

home from the hospital.

You've never been to that one. "I thought

I had been to all of them

with my mother," you think, but

this was the one where

everyone else went. Your sister

makes up a song in the car

about her new couch. You take turns

singing the made-up verses.

You drive past the water.

Do you go ahead

and laugh at the water?

Letter Poem #6

Dear February,

I know we'll be together again;
they can't stop us,
they don't even want to:
why would they even care?
There are too many buses,
no one can keep track of them all,
in winter, when they come up Main Street every fourth person.
Your purples—
how do I say it?
They are not even purple;
it's as though you make all the houses ugly again, *every day*—
god how I love that—
what you do with aluminum siding,
it's practically music—
it's like listening to a bus pull away—
If only you knew how it is
not to understand why seeing people's breath in the street
is not the same as snowing—
it's like chewing gum, smoking a cigarette,
getting cramps, throwing up,
making out in the dunes on the hillside above a chimney town.

Island

Finally you arrive at a small bungalow
with a thatched roof and bamboo frame.
Inside, is every face you've ever made. You
leave in a hurry, just go right back outside
and stand a few feet away with your back
to the door. Nearby, a gathering of
wives are seated at a bamboo
table. They wear suits and dainty shoes
and little anguish veils across their faces.
They have expensive, sharp silverware.
You wonder what will they eat?
As a special, expensive touch,
they have handmade White House
and Pentagon salt-and-pepper shakers. Why
do you feel sorry for them? A waiter
in a white jacket passes swiftly carrying
a silver-domed tray. You make a face
but you have no idea what
it is, and then you picture what face
you would make if you were someone
else. It's the "disgusted-and-relieved-
neighbor-over-the-garden-fence-I'm-glad-that's-not-
my-problem" face.
You figure both faces are going in the hut.
You wonder where in the hut will they go?
There was a group of faces that looked like

sorrow, and like envy, and indigestion, but
all at once, and they were marked
with peacock feathers; maybe these faces
went there. Or with the group that was labeled,
"Revulsion Exultation." Those faces
had crescent-moon eyes
and lips stretched to cry out without
a sound, a face that really starts
from the throat. Or maybe
it was a more contained sort of face,
like the ones called, "Mustache Skepticism";
it's like a string is pulling
one corner of the mouth, one nostril,
and the corner of one eye and
eyebrow. In those, you become
a skeptical man
with a dark mustache, even if,
in real life, you're a glamorous
marketing agent with the latest
pants and everything you do
makes little, delicate, sexual sounds,
like the sound of your wallet closing,
or your little high-heeled boots
coming down the hall. The wives
make little sounds like that,
and other ones. They're scraping
their cutlery on their plates

and every so often you have the feeling
that one of them hit the tines
of her fork against her front
teeth by accident, because she
couldn't really see through the
veil. You feel sorry for them.
You can't stand them. You
wish you were a marketing
agent. The waiter's name is
Mr. B. You go
into the women's room hut and
in the stall you make faces
that make you feel like
Mr. B until
you can weep like
him and as you weep
you peek through the stall
at the mirror at bald
eyes pleading something mottled
to themselves very close.

Not For Chopin

Don't put off your shower any more
listening to Chopin.
Take the Preludes personally;
he's telling you that he can describe a progression
that you yourself have been unable to see,
shapely, broad light at one-thirty,
evening traveling up a road,
an overcast day as gentle bones.
Don't remember the music;
remember it as something obvious
that you are compelled, doomed, to obscure
and complicate. You erase it twice.
The first time
as you listened, unable
to have it,
the second time
as you were unable
to remember it.
Angry with Chopin,
what does he know?
The components of your dinner are waiting for you downstairs.
The golden evening takes flat, slow turns outside.
Become gray.
Listen to him describe what you would be like

if you were blind, sitting in a chair, at a wake, the days short, that there might
     be nothing
else, night,
content, unable, unwishing, to recall desire, or sight.

From Speaking In The Fall

Was that the river?
No, it wasn't the river, oh, it was the sink.

We don't need a known reason, I say,

we can have our own ones;

we don't even have to know what they are;

they're from before all this,

they're from before everything,

from when the universe was a dark and cold place with nothing in it.

I feel that there is no telephone.

I see myself

as a cat who has learned how to imitate talking on the phone

through observation,

has learned how to pick up the receiver with its paw

and turns to look at the viewer

as though in mid-sentence; or maybe as a person

who has never seen a phone, and says blah blah blah

to the dial tone. The silence that once existed

in the dark cold universe: translated, the empty sound

is a place—the inside of the phone. Infinity,

I say, there it is.

This is where we all go to

when we touch each other;

this is what supernatural is.

I feel I can break

away everything. Today dark arrives

at a new hour.

Welcome, hour,

thank you

for transparenting yourself.

I will go quietly

into another room

into quietry

for you;

it'll just be us.

Because It Has To Be This Way

It's been a while since I've been so
blah blah blah, he says.
Blah blah, she says.

She thinks that the universe is expanding like a giant lily.

You don't know
these people. They're off
in a little theater. The set
is a bedroom with a modest
bed on which they lie. It's
lit with a bedside
lamp and rhythmic night sounds
come in from the dark
all around. He sleeps on his back
with his hands folded
demurely, waiting
to be exported by great forces.
She wonders if somewhere
there is a lake made of melted butter.
Outside the dark
the sky is golden-clouded
like a bible illustration. Jesus is there.
He's white, with a

chestnut beard and soft, brown eyes.
He's wearing a white robe.
His wounds are no longer
bleeding. He's doing a peaceful
pantomime, standing in the air,
two feet above the ground. And you know
what? He's really nice, and he has no
sense of humor. Or if he does,
it would have to do with
smiling and petting a deer, and
you feel like you might like each other
at first, but
you wouldn't. Jesus is hovering
in a green pasture, like in a storybook,
the one about the Country Mouse and
the City Mouse, which had a lovely
picture of the Country Mouse running
away over the hills, the smokestacks
soon small behind. He lets you run
over the green hills, and you never get tired.
He reaches out one arm
with his palm upturned, and raises it
towards the pasture. He tilts his chin
to the golden sky, like he's
singing, and taps his foot,
which is bare. Jesus has long nail beds
and a hairy big toe. Below,

the universe is forming other universes.

Jesus is doing an experiment. He needs to expand

right now. They'll mainly be used for storage.

Pool #13

I become envious
of my imagined image
of a person holding two six-shooters
and wearing clothes from the mall and a cowboy hat.
When I see *myself* like this
I see that I am ridiculous
and shameful;
I have never even held a gun,
or been on a horse—
I can see how badly
the day that I get on one will go;
a severed spine
at worst,
a day of sheepish fuck-ups at best.
Why is it so easy
for others to shoot guns and ride horses?
When I think of how unfair
this is, I'm infuriated.
As it is, the only solution
is to be pushed off a cliff;
that'll give the smack-down
to someone who gets excited
surrounded
by your own death-by-horse.

Pool #10

The cantaloupe lady is ringing my bell,
again. This should really stop. If I could,
I would wish that I could make her go away—
but the problem, the problem
is that *I don't think*
that it's her who's doing it:
I think it's the *melon*.
Everything is contingent
on its steady approach.
I don't think the sun will come up
unless it's possible
for the day to clear a path.
I think the best thing would be
for someone to beat me,
maybe with a stick,
until I say, "Day is night! Day is night!"

It Is Daylight

I called my house from a pay phone
down the street before I went home.
I needed to check on the empty situation.
It was daylight,
still here.
My shadow looked large and unschooled.
The sidewalk was yellow in the sun.
I was thinking that I wasn't anyone
and that my future would be a trajectory
leading further away.
The lilacs were out. They looked like a detail
from a bucolic story or tableau
where people are naked, eating picnics,
grapes, kissing, and drinking wine
while playing musical instruments. It seems made up,
but it's not. It must be based on a world
something like the one that's here while I'm walking.
Many houses are abutted by hedges.
I don't like this, but I wouldn't take them away.
The hedges are often surrounded by beds of woodchips.
The sight of them is a silent story about the dead.
I was filled with yearning
to sit against the side of a house

between two hedges.

I don't know how to pray but I would try.

I felt somber and excited about to go into my house.

Some people come down the street.

They're very dressed up.

I can see them from my bedroom window.

My house is quiet,

as though it isn't mine

but was given to me

by something other than myself.

The dressed up people cross the street

and walk under the lilac trees.

They look very nice and awful. The young woman

wears a peach dress with cream-colored heels.

She's with a young man wearing a dark blue suit

and a turquoise shirt. How unfortunate

that they have to go out in daylight

and see themselves

out among trees, streets, and open sounds.

Walking through my house, I love the doors

best. Waking up the other day, I went downstairs

and banged my face into the doorframe

of a closet. It hurt. It was only an accident,

but I ended up in tears.

Now with this bump on my forehead,

I'm grateful.

I wash the dishes, clean the bathroom, vacuum.

Over the course of several days

I feel satisfied that my apologies have run themselves out.

I don't know when it's time to stop

but eventually I do, and I do other things.

Garden Apartments

It was raining a little.
I wondered if I were outside
if I would get wet.
I was in the car.
I passed a school.
I didn't really know where I was.
I had lived near here for a while.
It was a quiet, residential neighborhood,
garden apartments in the back of the town.
I parked near a driveway and turned the car off.
They were basically ugly.
It's no one's fault though.
I wondered what I would do the rest of the day.
People were running their lives from here.
They had a coffee table and mugs with writing on them.
They had the rest of their lives. It was just like the other day.
The weather was warm for the first time.
I was out walking.
A young couple came out of a house.
She had just taken a shower,
blow-dried her hair and put make up on,
and put on light-colored pants and a t-shirt.
I smelled her shampoo
when they passed, and I felt afraid of the day.

The rest of the walk was better.

It smelled like rain in the car. There was no one around.

I heard my jacket when I moved.

I thought how god loves this place;

the grass was coming in, and the crocuses.

What if someone died, or got fired,

or vomited alone in the middle of the night?

The apartments were wood on the outside.

They were stained red like the color of a picnic table.

I was so ugly, I wasn't sure I'd even be able to drive.

April

It was hours before I sat down
with a bowl of soup, a soup
that I, myself made. I could not
decide which way to walk around
and approach the table
for the best outcome.
Morning was made up
of blather that sent me
to the outermost limits of slurping
on my fingers. Imagine,
trying to eat a soup without a spoon,
and all the time thinking
about the windows upstairs in the room
where I had sat working. What will become of us?
Once, I bought vegetables by the side of the road,
but that doesn't mean anything now. Now,
what I want now is raisins,
and I can't have any
unless I go to the store.
But I can't, because I'm writing a novel.
It's about a boy librarian
whose mother is very, very ill.
There is something in the freezer
marked "vanilla." I tasted it.

It was like ice cream, or like whipped cream.

But I became suddenly afraid

that it wasn't food, but poison

for the garden.

Now why would anyone do that?

The taste of it reminded me

of eating ice cream

after church or at a birthday party.

That the sun will rise again in the morning.

Children are so beautiful and adorable, it's a shame

about adorable adults,

that they always seem like untrustworthy alcoholics.

Money! When I think of my brothers

I haven't spoken to in years, I imagine

a map of the United States, and very hot days.

The amazing cemeteries

of grandparents and criminals

flank the April boulevards.

The sun comes up over New Jersey,

something I've seen once, from a car

after a night of rain and wind.

Pool #8

A gross exaggeration,
and a disgusting one, really.
The arc of beauty,
I was disappointed and relieved
to find out,
is an actual *rainbow*,
an actual *arc of beauty*.
How the sky was pink in the avenue
in the evening, everyone out walking
in their ugly clothes
under golden rooftops.
If I were someone else,
I would imagine them
with giant angel wings
like a vision
from a Jesus rock group,
the everyday evangelical
surrounding us in willing
or unwilling embrace,
the messiah to return
as a giant sympathy card.

January

A night fire,

and this one really burns the house down.

At dawn it's still smoking

and I love it so much,

like the world has happened the thing

I wanted;

not like it loves me, but like,

"I know, I *know*,"

it says, "calamity,"

like, "why not for you, too?"

and I feel so included and ordinary

like I know what real order is;

and like it exchanges a look with me

together as the sky gets lighter.

And too far

to hear I know

a rooster crows,

so far away it is gentle.

I am in love!

my heart sings to the trees,

as though they are full-leafed

among the bugs and flowers in June.

I am witness

that the inverse of this bare white morning

lives somewhere

beyond the blazes,

standing outside wrapped in a black and red plaid blanket.

I've never had a blanket like this before—

the fireman gave it to me;

it's the kind of thing that seems like other people,

that you might find in the trunk of someone's car,

or in their *chalet,*

and that they say *chalet* is a maudlin lie

that breaks your heart nevertheless,

thinking of gingerbread houses,

a hillside of yellow flowers,

a grown-up Heidi making sweet love to a boy named Heinrich;

it's like a blanket from a tv show

about a burning house.

Maybe I will run away with the fireman

what with all these new horizons—

it's only minutes though,

a couple of hours,

a next-day type feeling

after I spend all day wandering around town

in a blanket that looks like it came from Smokey the Bear,

or Smokey Stover,

or Paul Bunyan,

or Satan,

Satan with a wink,

that's the plaid;

in no time at all
I'm coming up the street
in the middle of the day,
coming somewhere
with a can of food
and a kitchen in my heart
thinking
the heart
can love anything,
cannot love anything.

Over No Hills

It civilizes me,

not like a private sense of bed

but that I have powers of speech at all—

I think I am going to stop

eating bits of paper

that don't say anything on them—

that don't even say anything on them—

I know I should do something

as they say, "for the snows of embarrassment"

like a day in March when the blood is closer,

day singing for the loss of its whip.

Closer, I say, *closer.*

Or maybe I'll arrange to have you run over by horses

unexpectedly.

At first it will seem terrible,

a wood-framed tableau in which you're torn limb from limb

or in what as a photograph an idiotic stranger will see and call "wild dust"

then ask about the car park,

something he says

that he brings out like a bow-legged cowboy walk

or leaning with one elbow on the counter.

He's our witness, how awful.

But eventually in our separate ways, we'll see the wisdom in it.

The horses are brown. They're from a painting

hanging in my once-room at the Hotel Phillips
in Bartlesville, Oklahoma.
When the next day I saw sunset on the prairie
it gave the impression that the world would go on
as only grassland.
It was my *wish*
not to know
its reach.
I looked at it like a dog,
a dog waiting to be shot
with a long rifle,
or just a double-barrel shotgun.
O sweet shotgun, make the sun go down.

Poem #9

And felt ashamed at this
clarity
though I've made a mess out of it
but knew
listening to the neighbor shovel
heavy ice in the driveway
and the sun was out
that it was a thing to go forward to;
Finally willing to talk to the trees,
maybe for the first time
ever
and like feeling ashamed
at what they would say to me;
confusion at the shrubs now looks good;
all the things that are called
that I don't know how they're called—
I'm brought to the low
approaching world below the upper air
contrite at how it continues
at my back,
while looking through the closet,
moving through the sheltered rooms
in the gentle passing of things I remember,
that I can stand still any moment in here

something will happen;

to think, now far away, about going down the beach road

past the marshes in late afternoon

and the marsh grass touched the edges of my eyeballs;

all the world inside this old afternoon

light won't become

come closer

stay there.

Heaven

It was finished and went to heaven.
Heaven is a white Formica table.
Not what I expected,
but I'm not unsatisfied.
God still isn't here.
I'm not even waiting.
Where would I be
trying to get to? It's like I'm a person
without face parts.
I remember what it was like
to use my eyes,
and the things I looked at.
I think a lot of seeing the world from a car,
being with the air over fields,
stable and light brown when it's gray out,
or invisible at night,
like they could be water
if you didn't know where you were;
and the different temperatures
from the window, and wearing clothes;
all converged in my irises
like something rising
but not moving,
that made the rest of me aware.

This is something like that,

except the rest of me isn't really part of it.

I put my hands on the table

and spread them, like

"here's all ten." There's nothing on it,

on the table,

so I found that out.

What did you do today?

I ask god.

God doesn't say anything.

I don't say anything else.

Not wanting to say anything,

I had that for a long time before,

and now it's here.

We stay like that

for a long time,

and I mean a really long time.

That's one thing,

god is the only one

who would do that.

West

A glass of orange juice

overpowers the counter.

The street in the window

is two minutes

into the future.

The past is out there,

but not as explicit.

If I move,

it's a small city

surrounded on one side by snow-carved peaks

restored from a poster in a public health facility; they're separated

from a desert in a bright, opaque,

amber shade that the make-up counter calls *Always*. I'm wearing

a peach turtleneck and menstruating

in a house with immaculate leather furniture.

The person I am now

who makes mention in the world

through an organized hair style,

but have not always been,

meets an unblemished wind

and lives

the kindness of normalcy.

At the neighbor's co-worker's house,

the guest half-bath

has silver and blue vinyl walls
with giant white flowers
like a Paleolithic nightclub
inside a dogwood tree.
The guest soap all but actually is
a small lemon,
but more fragrant and beautiful
without pungency, in this room,
the present?

Central Park South

The coffee rings are in view
on the papers and book covers; big news
in the rabbit hospital. You can see it:
the bunnies are bandaged around their heads. He has a fancy office
on Central Park South
on the other side of the carriage driveway
across from the Plaza, one block
from the green and stone
Park horizon
behind the cream and gold awning
at The Pierre, where he does your root canals
from a room on the periphery.
You hope he might adopt you.
You won't know until the end. He discusses your nerve endings,
the fate of your face, puppets
of a baby pig and a baby tiger
who become friends
in deep privacy
sequestered on a boat leaving for Denmark. They decide to stay
and suckle from separate mothers. In your senses
is mint,
petals, grass,
or water;
you awake

in the sweet air:

You are my endodontist.

It's not about goats and flowers;

subtle;

we can do this;

we do,

without thinking

about bodies of water or bodies

of land in the vicinity of the future

where you do not arrive

on time, or ever. He's in your teeth;

this is where you're going. You trust him

because he won't remember

unless you ask him. He knows your mother.

It was before she was born. The teeth in your mouth

are the first step

in a desert vacation

on a poster at a retailer for outdoor grills. You turn into the street;

a lampshade; a bathroom

with expensive hand towels; a lobby; there's almost nothing

you can't turn into: he's that good.

I want it to be permanent.

Well it is, he says.

Where are my molars? you say.

I'm not here;

I know, you say, you ask

about red carnations, why

they bring on the night,

upset internal

muscles, make your face

distorted, forthright, inseparable

from a life

yoked to the mantle

of state

violence

and love indistinguishable

from privacy.

The windows on the pews

turn from rain

dusk to night.

I can't see the air around my face;

it's not your fault,

he says: we're in the pain removal.

The pyramids were getting bigger, that was the reason,

you said. He stayed and finished; different work crews,

you never met. You have a heat source in your chest,

an electric space heater for office use only; it is, he said, it was;

I'm snowing;

I know, there was nothing

in sight, no edge

that couldn't be flown off of

with yellow wings and a prescription ad

meadow, no dog in the neighborhood

that didn't come around

in a friendly way at twilight. He ate your share of dinner

and counted your socks. This was the way

forward. In olden times,

it was a candle in a metal candle dish, a whistled tune, a small drape, delicate smoke,

dementia. Your DNA showed up on microfilm

in the middle of Chinese food in the kitchen

and he threw a ball through the neighbor's window, wiped out on his bike,

inhaled the night mist in a parking lot. There were several lifetimes:

log cabins, maple syrup, Daniel Boone, corpuscles of new sea life

pulsing the preternatural

parts of the future, the plantation, triage,

appliances, horse muscles. Your parents

are his parents'

parents' children, and his parents are his parents' children. You can never

meet, you are only four. You can't reach anything

in your kitchen and you can't read. The social worker calls

the librarians. There are times

it's lonely, but this is.

The yarn bathing costume and the burlap discussion

face hats are at the drycleaners. He won't be here

when you get back. He

is me

being me yelling at me

that this is our last five minutes together. There is

the airport, the sod farm, the sorghum auction, the coast, the long

hot summer, the deaths

to be witnessed, the pre-schoolers

to be consoled, amputees

to be rescued, the world's oldest children,

mud people, wagon wheel museum

in flames, every burning spoke

a hill. You run.

You are not on time at the same time

on the same day in Tenochtitlán and modern Newfoundland.

Your mother was a bucket

and her head appeared inside

with a command of nuanced gestures. Your hair caught on fire

one sad colonial night

inside the ruffled night cap. We were poisoned squirrels. I know,

he says,

by the tree. You were

born knowing the shape of his toenail; the coffee table is an homage.

He tried to help you remember,

that is his job: a bookshelf, a boot, a lasso, a can

of beans, a train, Italy, a cloud giving out

rain in a picture. You were mute: Mary Ingalls,

who strove to leave the blind school, loved the presents

Pa brought from Mankato for everyone and Ma: chocolate, paper,

and string in his pockets. We shared

our forbidden love on the banks of Plum Creek. You touched

yourself in back of the empty schoolhouse. He wasn't born yet,

will never be

born, you will

never be born, you said. You went out

to the parking garage,

found your car, left in winter,

ate blubber, cried your tears, stank

in furs and skins. He was the white man. You died

of bronchitis. Your mother was a cat. He bathed

in the river with the other boys

in the manner of the day. He was, and you asked him to be

in your face. You were hit

by a taxi

in the rain crossing the street when you saw him

the first time. He took you

to the hospital downtown.

Bed Poem

In the shower,
lunchtime.
It's nice not to be out with the cars,
and that there's nothing to hear
when I come out, either.
She's going out for carpaccio
and a musical tonight.
I'm having a piece of light that broke on a building
two weeks ago.
She's moving slowly; she allows me to watch her leave
to indicate that she's coming back. All I can think
is how nice it is without her. I'm about to lie down
in bed with the towels,
for as long as it takes. I don't really hope
she won't come back,
but I like to indulge it; I don't feel like
diagnosing plastic containers later,
or planning a group library day
with the hookers
on the next block.
Once, she made me bring three years'
worth of magazines to a shelter
for dogs. When we got home, we had to enter all their names
and personal information into a database

sorted to indicate their levels of at-risk behavior:

Poppyseed,

Savon, Cory,

Anne Boleyn,

Stiletto, Jackrabbit. It was like one winter

when I had to lick a hundred

holiday stamps

at work. Afterward, I was relieved

that I was still myself. I drove home at midnight,

but maybe it was only nine-thirty.

I was tired, so that was ok.

What did I have going anyway?

Plus I like the part when those things end.

She likes to do her job. What was all this "dividing things up

into preferences"? she asked. Why wasn't it all

part of the greater good?

Greater good?

"Futility is what's keeping the horses alive!" I joked.

I told her I'd be here if she needed me.

Elegy

She asks me if the great aunt has been around lately.

What do you mean by lately? I say.

I've been doing too much of this recently.

She doesn't say anything.

No, I tell her. No.

I think it's because I've been shirking my duties;

she thinks this.

Maybe she's right, or maybe she's not right at all;

we can't always agree;

I don't think I've seen her,

I say,

because she answered the question. Remember?

After the great aunt died,

I saw her all the time.

She never said anything,

which I assumed was a reflection of my own

failings. I decided she wasn't saying anything

because she was mad, at me,

and also in general. She was a kind and stubborn person when alive.

She had survived a genocide, and spent the back end of her life

in a small room, coming out to eat farina.

I wish this were not what I had to say,

but in spite of how things seem, or what I think

I might know otherwise,

the truth is that I know almost nothing

about any family members, because

I wasn't there for their lives. Stories

are not the same thing. As she got deeper into being dead,

she became—*tan;*

her white hair was longer,

and she didn't wear it up anymore. Based on a loosely conceived pre-colonial
    aesthetic,

I thought the new hairstyle made her look mannish. In life,

I have never seen her tan;

it occurred to me

that she must have

been tan, when the Turks marched her family across the desert;

but that's the only time I would know about. I never once saw her at a beach.

A dead person with a tan is worrisome:

had she

gone to hell?

That's impossible, I thought. *Genocide?*

Farina?

Doesn't she automatically get her ticket punched?

And that's assuming that hell is anywhere.

This is so stupid, I think,

This isn't—

—what?

This isn't what?

After I saw her a number of times,

starting in the predictable moss-covered stone chambers

and ending on an astringent deck of a ship

heading for probably

a Greek island with one olive tree on it,

I felt an urgent question forming.

I didn't know what it was though.

It came to me though: Is it better to be alive or dead?

She said "It's better alive."

Arctic Poem

The Goldilocks theory of the universe is in play.

The most important thing is not to exult.

The day after it snows

is reason itself.

The universe is on earth,

unexpurgated

soil and frost.

There's an empty pine tree

outside the door

with a piece of snow under it.

It's what you think it is. It has minuscule surface

black bits of softened wood and the road

and a space of grass

next to the cement walk.

It's after seven,

zero.

The linoleum carpet,

bag of sweat socks in my mouth.

It's cold this morning in the dog pile.

It's still dim. The air

is a thing of actual beauty,

it really is. I can see it from under my teeth. The lights are low

at Best Buy

in the Arctic.

The chandelier is still on.

Mounted snow to the end. Night halos

any time of day. If you take away all the light

there's a nebula in your face.

Pennsylvania

Pennsylvania,
my one and only
hell, the one
I know; periwinkle
gray vale, or dale, gentle
in spite
of a shadowed breeze; utterly
apprehensible, though there is no way, truly
to know
what its sky is: a pale vein
at the temple;
a separation from the land outside
by a gigantic
translucent bruise-colored petal
too big to see. If I had stayed
I wouldn't
know this was hell,
would I? But I drove
the mountains. I saw
a sixteen-year-old boy
steering a plow
next to the interstate
drawn by Clydesdales
with hooves like stones

for a house in a fable

about a past

that suggests to me,

as the head of a man with a horseshoe beard

floats out the backseat window,

that it and nothing else

belongs to me. Yellow meadow

from the windshield

having a coffee in the car. The dawn

of night traveling, pulling off

at a lamp-lit town

to eat pizza. I wanted to love

Pennsylvania, but it was cold

for May, like the end

of summer.

Night

inside a house without lights on. This is the place

where nothing

is meant for you.

I want

a life,

I said, remembering

a time when I lay down on the carpet.

But it doesn't matter

in Pennsylvania. There were wood clocks

and a cuckoo bird in the panoply; chests of drawers

engraved with acorns; silver-plated steins and coffee service trays; a silhouette

cut-out of a man

with a hulihee, posing

with the beagle's plaintive

candor in a painting of dogs

playing poker; a scrimshaw

vanity set; and the genital appurtenances

of nauticism: fruit-wood

telescopes; scale model boats; jaunty scenes

featuring a deeply pigmented ocean

and sailors dressed up

to woo

ladies in pannier skirts and mermaids

with emerald tails and pretty nipples

in the windows on the sidewalk

while the ghost

of Johnny Tremain

disappears into a woman's slim

philtrum in the sky. When I was a small child, I tried to

build a low stone wall

like ones I had seen

in my inner romanticism. I said that my wall

looked like Pennsylvania. One day, I saw

a life-sized wall

like mine. It was purple outside, again

in the car. My parents

said we were in Pennsylvania.

It's your wall, my sister said.

My life will end.

I hope that when it does,

I won't be sad about this.

The other day, I woke up

for what I hope

will be the last time

in Pennsylvania. It was early

and the room was blue. The eyes of the person

lying beside me

were also blue, and it was hard

to make out

the difference. The dawn

had opened. I got up from bed to go down

to the street from the storefront

apartment to be closer

to the yellow day beginning,

because the sun, even in the realm of Pennsylvania,

is still the sun, from the normal world.

In the street where there was nobody

there was still one man coming

and dragging his leg.

I smoked and looked across

down a side street with a chain link fence and an elongated

rose bush with a few very impressive

bright pink roses, and I thought a dog

would start barking

at the sprinklers starting

by a small athletic field. I saw it

as if I were seeing it

from the windows upstairs

over the street in the blue Pennsylvania room. That day

in New Jersey the highway brought the horizon. The noise of the air

was there, but not loud

all around.

The sun went down

over the fields from the car

windows rolled down through the dark. A black lake

and a blurry rowboat

next to a marsh grass

bush; a lit-up

pool; branches in a deep

white-flowered shrub; verdant, oneiric

grass; fragrant

chlorine; the filter and the air conditioner

going in the morning.

Evening

Outside he saw furnaces.

The crucial May light elucidated

the blossoms. They were translucent. They appeared

pink, to move slowly. The bench

in the bright grass before night, the man driving

in the downtown dressed

in an elaborate outfit,

but it was the afternoon

bright in a swath around the man inside the man's car. Over and over

he saw the beach and the water. He was always exhilarated

with nothing. The person was there

in the middle of saying this like he did

in the morning. He spoke in the sink. His blood beat

in his stomach. Something happened with the person.

I'm hungry, he said. He roamed

inside,

in the fine air across the hedges; his excitement

felt like an opening in the evening

and he wanted the person

to walk through it; the headlights moved over the country.

Dawn

1

Night, dawn
seashells
traveled on
a shore.

He slit a zoo
full of animals.
It was only one calf.
It turned out to be a person,
not a calf. The calf
made sounds.
Blood filled the grass,
the end of winter. Day
in the sun for the first
time looked like a star. There had been
frost in the dark. There wasn't a calf
or a person, there had been
no killing. He put his arms around
it, made up its soul.

2

He had killed so many
people, it should have been quiet.
The city was not beneath
anything. The air is so beautiful,
it looks like light. Flesh,
he said in the taxi
going home
from killing, is wishes;
every minute becomes
solid as the last one
becomes all of them.
I built a ragged person with my hands,
he said, passing the airport,
it was loud, his mouth from the sky in the road.

3

He hit the person in the face.
Now they were the same person.
He slaughtered a bear
for a meat roast party:
Gewürztraminer, whole sparrows,
a black tree
to break their skulls
into fields.

4

He went on an outing
where he had been lost before.
This was such a beautiful feeling,
he wanted to have it again and again.
The grass rose
into hills, and the air was turning
to pink.
I love it here, he said.
A horse nuzzled his cheek,
and he imagined
only blood opening to the outside.

5

It's wrong to kill.
That's why,
he explained to the person,
he was holding the person's
face and throat.
Nothing was supposed to happen,
not death and not pain. No one
should be doing anything right now,
that was what he was demonstrating
to the person, who didn't know:
this was an explanation.

6

The next time, it was different.
So few of us,
he said,
so few of us
transact
one thing, then something else; or,
or
cross the difficulty;
he hid in the bushes
smelling his knees.
He didn't know what they smelled of.
He tested his thoughts
about food, there was no
reason or tradition.

7

Blood in a pit.
He couldn't stand it.
There was generosity forever.
It smelled like walking into a dark foyer.
It could have been a summer night,
or it could have been twilight
when snow started. He had walked home
from so many places.
It was terrible
to know, and one day not know,
he lamented in the basement at the Rotary meeting,
but he was only imagining; none of the parts
brought him to his senses and he didn't believe
he had ever held himself that way.

8

He kicked the dust with his shoe.

Things weren't going the best.

It seemed like it was always like this.

Nothing was real and no one was around.

He tried to think.

He could go downtown

and rub his palms and face against the side of a brick building

and say,

I want to see what you really look like.

He would sit somewhere all night and eat pie.

9

A shoe by the roadside.
From the windshield
he couldn't see inside the sky, or the gray
and green that made him say "It's this one."
It looked like time,
like himself. He drove. The sky
made him think of numbers,
and he thought the world was made
from invisible numbers
that piled into soft particles,
granules, yes, no.

10

He sat with his bindlestick by the side
of the road. He ate beans out of a can
as though he was the luckiest person,
the only person to know the things
that were here upon today in his eyes
and breath, and in the senses of his soul.
A tromp l'oeil of dogs painted on the wall
of a powder room in New Jersey was
part of it, something he had seen
through the gray water in the grass. "Light"
did not appear just now to mean light as
he knew it; it was that everything that
was visible came through a procedure
illuminated under electrons.

11

Gentle, painful sound,

it's coming from his face.

He doesn't want to talk,

hates the air; it moves towards the same things,

beautiful night,

beautiful night again, best missed

from afar. He thinks his personhood

in the dark in a room is the same as the dark

inside a small bag or drawer.

12

A rose garden.

One turns up in every city

he goes to. He wondered what became of all the things

that never happened. What purpose

thought could possibly serve? He tried

to reduce the feeling

to test its validity,

played a song

like a person

inside his soul.

13

It was a slow rain.
He couldn't tell
his muscles
from the backseat
driving in the hills.
It was fathomable.
His mind was between
the air and the other
part of the air.
The hotel sheets were bleached,
and predicted good weather.
He didn't know what he did
in them. He loved
coffee and plants. When the granite
rose up on the highway after breakfast,
he felt violent joy.
He was only harmful then
like quartz, mica, hard
soot, sap; the vertical
rock face soared
through the mourning inside him.

Parts Of An Argument

I didn't know I had god until god was gradually not there over time. I don't feel abandoned. It is part of taking things as they come. You can't feel abandoned by something that isn't officially your province. Because I don't believe in god, I used to think I was lucky that god was there anyway. I noticed it when I looked at my lap, to fold out a napkin, or put my hands on the thighs of my pants. When I look at the sky, I know that the forceful feeling it produces is an interface of my mind with space and light, but I have trouble placing another entity in this configuration, even though there is a tacit feeling that there might be one there. The sky seems to contain something that we are made out of. Involuntarily, I try to communicate with it. I often think the sky is a dead end. When I experience the power of the sky, I sometimes think of Celine Dion singing. Then I'm disappointed by my own mind, and I think that nothing is going to happen that hasn't already happened. Even though this can't be true, it indicates possible limitations. When I die, I don't want the sky to be there. This probably isn't true. I have been lucky in traditional ways: I was not born into poverty, and all the parts of my body are in working condition. I realize that most people think it's pathetic to be grateful for those things, because life is about so much more. Unfortunately, this isn't true for me. It's as if someone, god, gave me a microwave oven, but I never took it out of the box because I was grateful and never touched it. At some point, waiting for me to open it, god probably realized that I was unable to appreciate the item, and decided that it was a mistake to have given it to me. I thought, mistakenly, that I *was* appreciating it: I thought about all the things I would be lucky enough to make: steamed squash; popcorn; tea; I could heat up spaghetti and meatballs, and left over Chinese food. At the same time though, I imagined that other people were either using their microwaves constantly for things I hadn't done: defrosting ice cream, and heating up leftovers from restaurants I couldn't afford; or they had returned their microwave for something else. I wondered what side of god was present in their lives that they had the freedom, or the sort of relationship with god where they could do this. I thought of Kissinger, and what appliance god had given him. Kissinger's appliance might have been a horse. Kissinger probably shot the horse, I thought, and I bet god understood why and secretly respected him for it. They probably had a sophisticated argument about it and then god would tell everyone that Kissinger is flawed and cruel, but that those who are sophisticated will understand the value of power and complexity. If I had thrown my microwave out the window a week after it arrived, I probably wouldn't be any worse off. In terms of results, god probably decided that things turned out the same. My mistake was that I thought the microwave was an imagining machine. I would rather imagine heating up spaghetti, and making squash, popcorn, and tea, because in reality, I don't eat this way. It sounds simple and fun, but it is still not a big deal to use pots on the stove. It reminds me of working in an office, something I've never liked. Maybe that's what god's gift is, maybe god thinks that I should work in an office. Or maybe god thinks that I should bear many children, because a large family situation is also useful for a microwave. By not opening the microwave, I was at the same time thanking god and using the gift in the best way that I could, while still considering the person I know myself to be, but I was also having an argument of sorts with god, but obviously not a sophisticated one on the order of Kissinger's argument with god. Maybe god really meant that I should work in an office and bear many children and eat microwave popcorn. I don't think this was god's intention though, because god had helped me escape exactly such a situation. I worked in an office with a microwave, and although I did not eat microwave popcorn, or use the microwave, I could have, and my job at this office supported the family setting in which I lived. This family setting became intolerable because of a great lie, and after a number of years, god gave me permission to reject the microwave oven. I was angry with myself for the way I had proceeded with the microwave, and angry with god that god had not given me this permission sooner. I wondered if I had opened the microwave and used it if I would have known sooner, with the certainty that I felt was necessary, that this family setting depended upon a colossal and undoable lie that damaged everyone who came into contact with it. I decided to run away from the lie before it destroyed me forever. I thought that god would support this decision, but god seemed to be of two minds about it, and that also made me angry.

In the time that I was angry, I thought of a huge sunset in the desert, which is a traditional image of the way that a notion of god interfaces with human spirituality. I thought that through the struggles of leaving the intolerable family setting and confronting the colossal lie, that I had advanced in life, and in the eyes of god, that we would now have a more sophisticated relationship like the one god had with Kissinger. Mostly though, I noticed that I could communicate better with god with the microwave in my foyer in its original factory packing. I liked having the original part of god's gift in my apartment. When I saw the box with blue writing printed on the outside and a pixilated drawing of a microwave with the company name on it, and the shipping label on it with the factory's address and my address, I thought about heaven. I don't believe in heaven, but I think heaven would have to do with acquiring knowledge like never before through interaction with the landscape and with other beings. What is so great about being in life though, is that you can lie down and breathe as a mammal in time, and I enjoy that. I enjoy using my eyes without the idea that my sight is for anything. The limited image is carried into my mind while I breathe. If I move my foot, so what? I'm an animal that moved its foot. None of it means anything in its parts, but accrues to something in the greatness of total time.

I used to be afraid of the time when the sun would end. I knew it was scientifically unlikely that it would stop in my lifetime, but it made life more frightening. I thought about the people who would be around when the sun was growing into a hot red giant, and how they would be uncomfortable and scorched. I felt frightened for them, at how trapped they would feel. And then, if there was anyone left, the ones who would be around when the sun started to shrink and cool down, and as it cooled the earth would be moving more and more slowly, making the days longer. For thousands of years we've lived in a peaceful feeling of an extant world, and for this we are truly lucky. It is a state of being embryonically lucky, lucky like a translucent form experiencing a quantum multiplication of its cellular advancement. It is a feeling of luck like drinking water from the faucet and wiping your face with your hands, and then wiping your face with a towel. Even if you are in your house, or in a restaurant bathroom using a paper towel, it can feel as though you are on the banks of an early river, close to the knowledge of your human origins, and a feeling like brightness moves between your organs and your eyes.

My personhood is primarily interested in making something out of nothing. If I could use the microwave to speak several languages and become a ballet dancer, I would do it. It is possible that if I continued to think about it, I would realize how.

Neptune

We pass the day in March of being in the cemetery and
        eating a burger.

The air is made out of statues and dead people.

This is why we have sex together.

Did I show you this?

It passed through the particles.

The shadow of a continent passed over
us like the shadow of a cloud over a body of water.

There is a picture of blowing out a ghost
and this is what life is like for the livers.

I wanted to ask you a bunch of things.

A sound curved inside a tall wave
that showed through on a gray morning one time;

How did you do it?

except it is still happening.

The white hovel projected from my insides,

out in the sun;

on the street in the snow,
the days move forward towards other things.

Soft day
with rain;

all common sense about the world,
the extent that anything is involuntary;
if your hands are on the rocks, your hands are on the rocks.

A cold aired-out smell restores time.
Trees, wine, and night on
the road in the car,
the inside of
hair, a blue mug, and a black couch.

In my dreams makes two,
under the duvet on the floor with the overhead light on,

after showering in the kitchen inside the dark windows.

It is night in Norway,
and outside the solar system.
It was as if

I was reaching my arms out towards you in darkness
but you are behind me.

It's twilight in the fourth dimension,
without sun, so it can never go down.
It is always night inside the neutrino.

The Gods are angry,
or they are excited?
The ocean is rising
from a picture about Neptune.
Neptune brings a man out of the sea.
The man is there. He tells me to come
find him while I'm dreaming.
I do that.
When we see each other,
we wait for some instructions.
There aren't any,
then there are;
we are naked
just like in real life.

A day and hours,
sky moves together.
The two gray skies move through my mind and the larger space
that makes my mind.
You are in some versions of them,
and sometimes in none of them.

The upstairs room in the summer is soft and quiet.

Rain dims coming in the night outside.

It is real that it is quiet, and the noise
is away from here, inside the train.

When I lie next to you I miss the world.

This is the beginning.

Here is one from that time.

It's morning on land with the blinds down. Your bones move forward through time towards the outside.

Poem

If only we knew what our choices were,

something besides being flogged.

I can't say I mind being flogged,

but I also don't do much else.

Yesterday it was as though I was back with the old watering can,

watering the tree out the window,

thinking about the old church

where all my memories began and are stored.

The happiness of an ordinary day on Twenty-Seventh Street!

Two-thirty, fifty degrees, partly cloudy.

An old Tuesday afternoon

in which nothing happens.

An old Tuesday

between the past and the future,

in which all of history's old strife has been long since laid down.

All the horses and brass shields, pointy spears and metal things

retired into relief

in copper, housed in a church,

starvation, pillaging, decapitation, and murder—

the way when you think of it,

you want to have your tongue ripped out of your head

and your insides punctured

and be left bleeding out of your mouth somewhere.

Instead it's so far away it is elegant,

it seems *human,*

even involves some sort of *piety*

as though in our hearts we are clothed in a plain smock

and dirty skin,

plain—

nothing possible.

The Sky As With Bells, As With Nothing In It

This bright day all together we eat a Sunday dinner.
We watch the sun in the wind through a mirror
that reflects the leaves blowing hard behind glass doors.
Yellow-green, turning violently and violently, and quiet.
The gilded mirror opens up to trees like a high gate
on a wall that leads nowhere, as to a room that lies behind—
a display for window curtains in a department store—
a window dressed up in its Sunday best, an organdy veil
under wool drapes, silky tie-backs with tassels, wall to wall carpet.
A light comes through the curtains as though the last afternoon rays
were coming through the curtains. The light that shines
from a small fixed bulb fixed to white sheet rock.

Come sunshine, finish powdering your nose.
The wind is colder, doors shrink in their frames and close louder.

Snow On The Apples

There was snow on the apples
somewhere.
You're at home,
it's getting dark out, rain
makes the cars louder. Nobody
seems to be driving
the cars. Someone has arranged
for them to be there going by,
six o'clock. Someone has made
the sound of air in the room louder.
God? you say, but not aloud. Since
there is no god, you have to be
both you and god. Yes, god says. You
turn over on the couch
and push your face into the dark.
Remember
when we went swimming?
The lakes, god says,
the one that was muddy
on the bottom, and the one you didn't like
that was too small; the one
when it was too cold, but he wanted
to go in before it rained; the one

with the floating dock in the middle
that reminded you of a drowning story?
That swimming, you say. God is quiet
for a minute; god is listening
to the news;
you listen too, even though
you're too tired to turn over
and watch. The story is
something about a fire
and a kidnapped boy.
They're interviewing the mother.
It was her boyfriend, they think,
she thinks. His name is Gerard
Stevens. They must be showing a picture
of him now, in case anyone knows
of his whereabouts. She's not
quite hysterical; why
doesn't she just start screaming
that that Gerard stole her little son
and now she's going to run away
into the local news trees
in the background and
eviscerate herself?
She's telling the tv reporter
in a head voice that sounds like
a piece of slaughterhouse machinery

that she's hoping the police will find her

son. Her voice makes you hungry.

You ask god if god

is hungry, and god is. You ask god

what you should do

for dinner, and god reminds you

that you have turkey burgers

in the freezer, and some broccoli.

You'll get up

with creases on your face.

The windows will be dark. You'll

go take the burgers out

and separate them with a knife.

They'll be slippery and frozen, and

you'll think of driving on an

icy road; and then

you'll put them in foil under

the broiler and start the water

for the broccoli, and take out

a plate for yourself, and get

the salt and pepper, and by

that time, god will have left.

God's going to a dinner

where they're having lamb chops

and veal stuffing with

roasted almonds and fig sauce and